Foreword

Welcome to Growth Mindset and congratulations on your decision to purchase this book.

This book is based on two highly popular books that approach improving mindset from different angles.

Part one of this book is based on making wise decisions in life while part two focuses on creating the mindset that happiness requires.

You may choose to follow the format of the book (one story lesson a day) or read at your own preferred pace . The true benefit will be found in the application of these lessons. With that being said, sit back, enjoy and ponder the following story lessons.

Table of Contents

Part 1: Get Wise..1

Introduction To Part 1...2

Day 1...4

Day 2...5

Day 3...7

Day 4...8

Day 5...9

Day 6...10

Day 7...12

Day 8...14

Day 9...15

Day 10...16

Day 11...18

Day 12...19

Day 13...22

Day 14...23

Day 15...25

Day 16...26

Day 17...27

Day 18...28

Day 19...30

Day 20...31

Day 21...32

Day 22...33

Day 23...35

Day 24...37

Day 25...39

Day 26...40

Day 27...42

Day 28...43

Day 29...44

Day 30...45

Conclusion to Part 1 47

Part 2: Get Happiness...48

Introduction To Part 2 49

Day 31...50

Day 32...51

Day 33...53

Day 34...55

Day 35...57

Day 36...59

Day 37...60

Day 38...62

Day 39...63

Day 40...64

Day 41...66

Day 42...67

Day 43...69

Day 44...71

Day 45...72

Day 46...74

Day 47..75

Day 48..76

Day 49..77

Day 50..78

Day 51..79

Day 52..81

Day 53..82

Day 54..83

Day 55..85

Day 56..86

Day 57 87

Day 58..88

Day 59..90

Day 60..91

Conclusion...93

Part 1: Get Wise

Wisdom to improve decision making & emotional intelligence for success in the modern world.

Introduction To Part 1.

"Tell me a fact and I'll learn. Tell me a truth and I'll believe. But tell me a story and it will live in my heart forever."

Part 1 features selected timeless tales of wisdom that can be applied today to help you make better decisions in business, your relationships and your outlook on life. The lessons taught are as applicable in our modern world as they were in the time they were created.

It has long been known that highly successful people will agree that being "street smart" is far more important to success than being "book smart".

Tony Robbins famously said "we are drowning in knowledge but starving for wisdom" and it's truer today than ever before. Our modern world places much value on learned factual knowledge while discounting experiential life knowledge.

Stories are the best way to transmit this form of knowing. Stories shape our perception of the world, and create the morality we live by. Stories also teach the fundamentals of living a good life better than moral precepts and instructions.

Some well known stories have been included. I encourage you not to skip over any stories, should you find that you have heard them already. It may just be the retelling of a story which may reveal to you a whole new level of understanding given your current situation in life.

Each of these stories have been left without interpretations. Related quotes have been included to provide extra food for thought. This allows you as the reader to ponder and draw your own meaning from each of these stories.

At least one story a day is recommended. Allow each story to penetrate deep and dwell in the depths of your mind. Do this and I wholeheartedly believe that you will see benefits in all areas of your decision making and disposition.

Day 1

Focus on improving your self first.

There was once a pair of acrobats. The teacher was a poor widower and the student was a young girl named Meda. These acrobats performed each day on the streets in order to earn enough to eat.

Their act involved the teacher balancing a tall bamboo pole on his head while the little girl climbed slowly to the top. Once at the top, she remained there while the teacher walked around.

They both had to keep complete focus and balance to prevent any injuries and complete the performance. One day, the teacher said to the pupil:

"Listen Meda, I will watch you and you watch me, so that we can help each other improve, maintain concentration and balance to prevent an accident. Then we'll surely earn enough to eat."

The little girl was wise however and answered,

"But dear master, I think it would be better for each of us to watch and improve ourself. To improve and look after oneself means to look after both of us. That way I am sure we will avoid any accidents and earn enough to eat."

"Make the most of yourself....for that is all there is of you."

— Ralph Waldo Emerson

Day 2

Practise non-judgement & open-mindedness in all things.

I. Once, there was an old farmer who had worked his crops for many years. One day his horse ran away. Upon hearing the news, his neighbours came to visit.

"Such bad luck," they said sympathetically.

"Maybe," the farmer replied.

The next morning the horse returned, bringing with it three other wild horses.

"How wonderful," the neighbours exclaimed.

"Maybe," replied the old man.

The following day, his son tried to ride one of the untamed horses, was thrown, and broke his leg. The neighbours again came to offer their sympathy on his misfortune.

"Maybe," answered the farmer.

The next day, military officials came to the village to draft young men into the army. Seeing that the son's leg was broken, they passed him by. The neighbours congratulated the farmer on how well things had turned out.

"Maybe," said the farmer.

II. A student went to his meditation teacher and said,

"My meditation is horrible! I feel so distracted, my legs ache, and I'm constantly falling asleep. It's just horrible!"

"It will pass," the teacher said matter-of-factly.

A week later, the student came back to his teacher.

"My meditation is wonderful! I feel so aware, so peaceful, so alive! It's just wonderful!'

"It will pass," the teacher replied matter-of-factly.

"Go through life with an open-mind and you will find a lot of open doors"

Day 3

<u>Maintain freedom above all else.</u>

A gaunt Wolf was almost dead with hunger when he happened to meet a House-dog who was passing by.

"Ah, Cousin," said the Dog.

"I knew how it would be. Your irregular life will soon be the ruin of you. Why do you not work as I do, and get your food regularly given to you?"

"I would have no objection," said the Wolf, "if I could only get a place."

"I will easily arrange that for you," said the Dog; "come with me to my master and you shall share my work."

So the Wolf and the Dog went towards the town together.

On the way there the Wolf noticed that the fur on part of the Dog's neck had worn away, so he asked him what had happened.

"Oh, it is nothing," said the Dog. "That is only the place where the collar is put on at night to keep me chained up; it chafes a bit, but you soon get used to it."

"Is that all?" said the Wolf. "Then good-bye to you, Master Dog."

"Freedom lies in being bold"

- Robert Frost.

Day 4

Feed good habits, starve bad habits.

An old Cherokee chief was teaching his grandson about life...

"A fight is going on inside me," he said to the boy. "It is a terrible fight and it is between two wolves.

One wolf is evil. He is anger, envy, sorrow, regret, greed, arrogance, self-pity, guilt, resentment, inferiority, lies, false pride, superiority, self-doubt, and ego.

The other wolf is good, he is joy, peace, love, hope, serenity, humility, kindness, benevolence, empathy, generosity, truth, compassion, and faith.

This same fight is going on inside you, and inside every other person, too."

The grandson thought about it for a minute and then asked his grandfather,

"Which wolf will win?"

The old chief simply replied, "The one you feed."

"Successful people are simply those with successful habits. "

Day 5

Bad habits grow in strength, eradicate them early.

A wealthy man sought the help of a wise man to help wean his son away from his bad habits.

The wise man took the young boy for a stroll through a garden. Stopping suddenly he asked the boy to pull out a tiny plant growing there.

The boy held the plant in his hands and pulled it out.

The old man then asked him to pull out a slightly bigger plant. The youth pulled hard and the plant came out, roots and all.

"Now pull out that one," said the old man pointing to a bush. The boy had to use all his strength to pull it out.

"Now take this one out," said the old man, pointing to a guava tree. The boy held onto the trunk and tried to pull it out. But it would not budge.

"It's impossible," said the boy, panting with the effort.

"And so it is with bad habits," said the wise man. "When they are young it is easy to pull them out, but when they take hold they cannot be uprooted."

It was this stroll with the wise man which changed the boy's life forever.

"To change your life, change your thought habits."

Day 6

Recognise and remove old faulty ways of thinking.

I.   Once there were two ants sitting on the rim of a cup that contained amrit, the nectar of immortality.

As they were talking, one of the ants lost his balance and was about to fall into the cup. He somehow managed to get back on the rim. The other ant asked him,

'Why don't you want to fall into the cup? Even if you drown in this, you will become only immortal.'

The first ant replied, 'But I don't want to drown!'

II.   Once there were two ants. One lived in a sack of salt while the other lived nearby in a sack of sugar. The sugar ant once visited her neighbour and tasted the salt in her sack. Finding it bitter she said,

"Do come and visit my house. I'm sure you'll find the food there much to your liking."

The salt-fed ant accepted her neighbour's invitation. Being naturally cautious and not wanting to run short of food she took a grain of salt with her in her mouth.

When she ate the sugar she said,

"Frankly I don't know what you're talking about. Your food tastes much like mine."

The sugar fed ant replied,

"Perhaps that's because you're holding onto something of your own. Get rid of that and I'm sure you'll notice the difference."

The salt fed ant cleaned out her mouth, tasted the sugar and never returned to the sack of salt.

"Old ways won't open new doors"

Day 7

Get uncomfortable in order to succeed

A Monk set out on his travels accompanied by his assistant, a Brother. As it was getting dark the Monk told the Brother to go on ahead to find lodging. The Brother searched the deserted landscape until he found a humble shack, in the middle of nowhere.

A poor family lived in the shack. The mother, father and children were dressed in rags. The Brother asked if he and the Monk could spend the night.

"You are most welcome to spend the night," said the father of the family.

The poor family prepared a simple meal consisting of fresh milk, cheese and cream for the Brother and the Monk. The Brother felt moved by their poverty and even more by their simple generosity.

After eating, the Monk asked them how they managed to survive in such a poor place, so far away from the nearest neighbours and town. The wife looked to her husband to answer. In a resigned tone of voice he told them how they managed to survive.

"We have one cow. We sell her milk to our neighbours who live nearby. We hold back enough for our needs. We make cheese and cream and that is what we eat."

The next morning, the Brother and the Monk said their goodbyes and set out to continue their journey.

After walking a few miles, the Monk turned to the Brother and said, "Go back and push the cow off the cliff!"

"Father," the Brother replied, "they live off the cow. Without her, they will have nothing."

The Monk repeated his order "go back and kill the cow." With a heavy heart, the brother returned to the old shack. He worried about the future of the family because he knew they depended on the cow to survive. Bound by a vow of obedience he followed the monk's orders and pushed the cow off the cliff.

Years later, the young Brother became a Monk. One day he found himself on the same road where he had found the shack so many years ago. Driven by a sense of remorse he decided to visit the family. As he came around the corner he saw a splendid mansion, surrounded by landscaped gardens, in the place where the shack used to be. The new house exuded a sense of prosperity and happiness.

The Monk knocked on the door. A well-dressed man answered. The Monk asked, "what ever became of the family who used to live here? Did they sell the property to you?" The man looked surprised and said he and his family had always lived on the property. The Monk told him how he had stayed in a shack on the same spot, with his master the old Monk.

The man invited the Monk to stay with him as his guest. While they ate, the host explained how the family's fortune changed. "You know Father, we used to have a cow. She kept us alive. We didn't own anything else. One day she fell down the cliff and died. To survive, we had to start doing other things, develop skills we did not even know we had."

"We were forced to come up with new ways of doing things. It was the best thing that ever happened to us! We are now much better off than before."

"If you always do what you always did, you will always get what you've always got."

"There is wonder to see, to feel and to enjoy awaiting the moment you choose discomfort."

Day 8

Necessity creates resourcefulness

A CROW dying from thirst saw a large cup, and hoping to find water, flew to it with delight.

When he reached it, he discovered to his grief that it contained so little water that he could not possibly get at it.

He tried everything he could think of to reach the water, but all his efforts were in vain.

At last he collected as many stones as he could carry and dropped them one by one with his beak into the cup, until he brought the water within his reach.

He thus saved his life.

"Discontent is the first necessity of progress."

-Thomas Edison.

"Necessity may be the mother of invention, but "play" is certainly the father"

- Roger Von Oech.

Day 9

Everyone needs to eat.

The BIRD-CATCHER was about to sit down to an unimpressive dinner of herbs when his friend unexpectedly visited.

Being the good host he was, it was his duty to also provide dinner for his friend as well. However, his regular source of food, his bird trap had been empty for quite some time. He therefore decided it wise to kill his Pied Partridge, which had been used as a decoy.

The Pied Partridge exclaimed "What would you do without me when next you spread your nets? Who would chirp you to sleep, or call for you a flock of answering birds?"

The Bird-catcher spared the Pied Partridge's life.

He then turned his attention to his rooster. The Rooster exclaimed "If you kill me, who will announce to you the appearance of dawn? Who will wake you to your daily tasks or tell you when it is time to visit the bird-trap in the morning?"

The bird-catcher replied, "It is true. You are a great bird at telling the time. But, my friend and I must eat."

"Necessity knows no laws except to conquer"

- Publilius Syrus

Day 10

Depend on no-one but yourself.

I. One day an ordinary man decided to finally reach for his dream. However he didn't believe he had enough strength to achieve it. He turned to his mother: "Mother, help me!"

"Darling, I would love to help but I am unable. Everything I have, I already gave to you..."

He asked a wise man:

"Master, please tell where I can gain strength?"

"It's said to be found on Mount Everest. However I found nothing there except snowy winds and lost time"

He asked the hermit:

"Holy Father, where may I find the strength required to attain my dream?"

"In your prayers my son. If your dream is false, you will find peace in your prayers..."

The man asked everyone, but all he found was confusion.

"Why are you so confused?" asked an old man passing by.

"I have a dream, good man. But I don't know where to find strength for its realisation. I asked everyone, but no one could help me."

"No one?" said the old man with a sparkle in his eyes,

"And did you ask yourself?"

II.   A merchant was once driving a heavy load along a very muddy way.   He came to a part of the road where the wheels sank half-way into the muddy road, and the more the horses pulled, the deeper sank the wheels.

So the merchant threw down his whip, and knelt down and prayed to Hercules the Strong.   "Hercules, help me in my hour of distress." But Hercules appeared to him, and said:

"Man, don't sprawl there. Get up and put your shoulder to the wheel."

"Depend on no one but yourself. Even our shadow leaves us in the midst of darkness"

"Self sufficiency is the greatest of all wealth" - Epicurus

"Happiness belongs to the self-sufficient" - Aristotle

Day 11

One does not need many friends, just a few true friends.

A Hare was very popular with the other beasts who all claimed to be her friend. One day she heard the sound of hounds approaching.

Hoping to escape with the help of her many friends she went to the horse, and asked him to carry her away from the hounds on his back. The horse declined, stating that he had important work to do for his master. He felt sure, he said, "that her many other friends would come to her assistance." She then applied to the bull, hoping he would repel the hounds with his horns. The bull replied: "I am very sorry, but I have an appointment with a lady. I am sure that our friend the goat will help you."

The goat, however, feared that the hare might do his back some harm if he took her upon it. The ram, he felt sure, was the proper friend to apply to. So she went to the ram and told him the case. The ram replied: "Another time, my dear friend. I do not like to interfere on the present occasion. Hounds have been known to eat sheep as well as hares."

The Hare then applied, as a last hope, to the calf, who regretted that he was unable to help her, as he did not like to take the responsibility upon himself, as so many older persons than himself had declined the task. By this time the hounds were quite near. The hare took to her heels and luckily escaped.

"People are more what they hide than what they show"

"To make a hundred friends is not a miracle. The miracle is to make a single friend who will stand by your side even when hundreds are against you.

Day 12

Create powerful and true friendships

I. A prince and the minister's son were out hunting in the forest. Hungry and exhausted after a long day's wandering they rested in the shade of a tree. The prince soon fell asleep, while the minister's son stayed awake and kept guard.

A snake soon slithered towards the prince. Hissing furiously, it prepared to bite him. The minister's son was quick. He raised his sword. But before he could kill the snake it said "This prince was my enemy in my past life. I cannot rest until I drink blood from his neck."

The minister's son wanted to save his friend's life and he was also intelligent. "Then, what if I give you some of his blood to drink. Will that quench your hate?" He knew that if blood was all the snake wanted then he could easily save his friends life, as long as he were the one to give it. For if the snake were the one to draw blood then it would at the same time spit poison that would surely to kill his friend. The snake agreed. He was only after the prince's blood, not his life.

The minister's son made a cup out of dry leaves. He climbed upon the chest of the prince who was still fast asleep. He pulled out his dagger and made a small slit on the side of his neck. The sharp cut suddenly shocked the prince awake. But on seeing that his friend, was the one holding the dagger, he closed his eyes again.

The minister's son filled the cup with enough blood and offered it to the snake, which drank the blood and went its way. Meanwhile, he collected some medicinal herbs and bandaged the wound.

A few hours later, the prince awoke and made preparations to proceed further. He said nothing and walked happily as if nothing had happened. Two whole days passed in the forest, yet the prince never reminded him of the event.

It was the minister's son who began to grow impatient, as to why he was not questioned.

He finally said, "Friend and master, you know that I climbed upon you and slit your throat, drew blood and then bandaged you. You even saw me do it. Still why haven't you questioned me and asked for an explanation?"

"You are a dear friend," the prince answered. "I believe that whatever you may have done must have been for my good. This is why I need no explanation." He continued, "If someone else had attempted this, then surely the case would have been different. You're a true friend and I have boundless trust in you.

A true friend is he who is harsh in order to bring about greater good. In return, a true friend does not sulk or feel hurt by the actions of his friend.

II. An Ant visiting a river to drink, fell in and was carried along in the stream.

A Dove pitied her condition, and threw into the river a small stick, by means of which the ant made its way to the shore.

The Ant afterward, seeing a man with a bow and arrow, aiming at the Dove, stung him on his foot sharply. The man missed his aim, and so saved the Dove's life.

"In life we never lose friends, we only learn who our true friends are"

"A true friend is the best possession"

Day 13

Forgive people, forget bad feelings, but most importantly: always be learning.

There was once a Master who while a boy at school, was treated with persistent cruelty by a classmate..

Now, older and remorseful the classmate came to the monastery and was received with open arms.

One day he brought up the subject of his former cruelty, but the Master seemed not to recall it.

"Don't you remember?" said the visitor

"I distinctly remember forgetting it!" said the Master, and with that they both melted with innocent laughter.

"Let no man pull you low enough to hate him" - *Martin Luther King JR*

"The weak can never forgive. Forgiveness is an attribute of the strong" - Ghandi

"Forgiveness is a gift you give yourself" - Tony Robbins

"True forgiveness is when you can say; thank you for that experience" - Oprah

Day 14

Keep only good company

I.   A man who wanted to buy a donkey went to market. Coming across a likely-looking beast, he arranged with the owner that he should be allowed to take him home on trial to see what he was like.

When he reached home, he led his new donkey into his stable along with the other donkeys. The new donkey looked around, and immediately went and chose a place next to the laziest and greediest donkey in the stable.

When the master saw this he put a halter on his new donkey at once, and returned the donkey to his owner again.

The owner was surprised to see him back so soon, and said, "You have tested him already?"

"I don't want to put him through any more tests," replied the man. "I could see what sort of animal he was from the companion he chose for himself."

II. A sick deer lay down in a quiet corner of a field. Many of his friends came in great numbers to offer their sympathies. A small number of his true friends brought with them food to ensure the deer's survival and placed it at the sick deer's feet.

A greater number of the sick deer's friends also visited but came empty handed. Each of them helped themselves to a small share of the sick deer's food, thinking no harm could come of such a small portion. Eventually the sick deer died not from his sickness, but from starvation.

"If you lie down with dogs you get up with fleas" - Benjamin Franklin

"One cannot spend time with negative people and expect a positive life"

Day 15

Expand the edges of your mind

An aging master had a student who constantly complained. So, one morning, the master sent him for some salt.

When the student returned, the master asked him to put a handful of salt in a cup of water and then drink it. "How does it taste?" the master asked.

"Bitter" spit the student.

The master chuckled and then asked the student to take the same handful of salt and put it in the lake.

The two walked in silence to the nearby lake. The student swirled his handful of salt in the water, the old man said, "Now drink from the lake." As the student drank from the lake, the master asked, "How does it taste?" "Fresh," he remarked. "Do you taste the salt?" asked the master. "No," said the student.

The master then sat alongside his student who reminded him of his younger self and said: "The pain of life is pure salt; no more, no less. The amount of pain in life remains the same, exactly the same. But the amount of bitterness we taste depends on the container we put the pain in. So when you are in pain, the only thing you can do is to enlarge your sense of things. Do not be a cup. Become a lake."

"If you change the way you look at things, the things you look at change" - Dr Wayne Dyer

"The only people who see the whole picture are the ones who step out of the frame" - Salman Rushdie

Day 16

Happiness lives both in the journey and acceptance.

There was once an old Chinese woman whose only son had just died. In her grief, she went to the holy man and asked, "What prayers, what magical incantations do you have to bring my son back to life?"

Instead of sending her away or reasoning with her, he said to her, "Fetch me a mustard seed from a home that has never known sorrow. We will use it to drive away the sorrow in your life."

The woman went off at once in search of that magical mustard seed. She came first to a splendid mansion, knocked at the door, and said, "I am looking for a home that has never known sorrow. Is this such a place? It is very important to me." "You've certainly come to the wrong place," they told her and began to describe all the tragic things that had recently befallen them.

The woman thought to herself, "Who is better able to help these poor, unfortunate people than I, who have had misfortune of my my own?" She stayed to comfort them, and then went on in search of a home that had never known sorrow.

But wherever she turned, in hotels and in other places, she found one tale after another of sadness and misfortune. The woman became so involved in helping others cope with their sorrows that she eventually let go of her own.

It was then she realised that it was her journey to find the magical mustard seed that drove away her suffering and returned her happiness.

"Maybe it's not about the happy ending, maybe it's about the story"

Day 17

Don't complain, your experience will be more joyful because of it.

The monastery on Mount Serat in Spain requires much discipline. One of the requirements of this religious order is for the young men to maintain silence.

Opportunities to speak are scheduled once every two years, at which time they are allowed to speak only two words.

One young initiate in this religious order, who had completed his first two years of training, was invited by his superior to make his first two-word presentation. "Food terrible," he said.

Two years later the invitation was once again extended. The young man used this forum to exclaim, "Bed lumpy."

Arriving at his superior's office two years later he proclaimed, "I quit."

The superior looked at this young monk and said, "You know, it doesn't surprise me a bit. All you've done since you arrived is complain, complain, complain.

"If you cannot be positive, then at least be quiet" - *Joel Osteen*

"Never complain and never explain" - Benjamin Disraeli

Day 18

Spend your words wisely

I.   A woman whose tongue was sharp and unkind was accused of starting a rumour. She was brought before the village rabbi protesting,

"What I said was in jest ... just humor! My words were carried forth by others. I am not to blame."

But the victim cried for justice, saying,

"You've soiled my own good name!"

"I can make amends," said the accused woman, "I'll just take back my words and assume I'm excused." The rabbi listened to what she said, and sadly shook his head, "This woman does not comprehend her crime, she shall do it again and again in time."

And so he said to the accused woman, "Your careless words cannot be excused until ...You bring my feather pillow to the market square. Cut it and let the feathers fly through the air. When this task is done, bring me back the feathers ...every one."

The woman reluctantly agreed. She thought, "The wise old rabbi's gone mad indeed!" But to humor him, she took his pillow to the village square. She cut it and feathers filled the air.

She tried to catch. She tried to snatch. She tried to collect each feather. But weary with effort she clearly discovered, the task could not be done. She returned with very few feathers in hand.

"I couldn't get them back, they've scattered over the land!" she sighed as she lowered her head,

"Just like the words I can't take back, from the rumour I spread."

II.   A long time ago there was a boy. He was smart, talented and handsome. However, he was very selfish and his temper was so difficult, that nobody wanted to be friends with him. Often he got angry and said various hurtful things to people around him.

The boy's parents very concerned about his bad temper. They considered what they could do and one day the father had an idea. He called his son and gave him a hammer and a bag of nails. The father said: Every time you get angry, take a nail and drive into that old fence as hard as you can."

The fence was very tough and the hammer was heavy, nevertheless the boy was so furious that during the very first day he has driven 37 nails.

Day after day, week after week, the number of nails was gradually decreasing. After some time, the boy started to understand that holding his temper is easier that driving nails into the fence.

One day the boy didn't need hammer and nails anymore as he learned to hold his temper perfectly. So he came to his father and told about his achievement. „Now every time, when you hold your temper all day long, pull out one nail".

Much time has passed. At last the boy could be proud of himself as all the nails were gone. When he came to his father and told about this, he offered to come and take a careful look at the fence. „You did a good job, my son, but pay your attention to the holes that left from the nails. The fence will never be the same. The same happens when your say hurtful things to people, as your words leave scars in their hearts like those holes in the fence.

"Be sure to taste your words before you spit them out"

Day 19

To say more say less.

For days a couple traveled almost without speaking. Finally they arrived in the middle of the forest, and found the wise man they were searching for.

"My companion said almost nothing to me during the whole journey," said the young woman.

"A love without silence is a love without depth," answered the wise man.

"But he didn't even say that he loved me!"

"Some people always claim that. And we end up wondering if their words are true."

The three of them sat down on a rock. The wise man pointed to the field of flowers all around them.

"Nature isn't always repeating that God loves us. But we realize that through His flowers."

"Have more than you show, say less than you know"

"The less people know the more they yell" - Seth Godin

"Say less, mean more"

Day 20

What is held inside will always be displayed to the outside world.

Teacher: "If I were to squeeze this lemon as hard as I could, what would come out?"

Student: "Juice, of course."

Teacher: "Do you think orange juice could come out of it?"

Student: "Of course not. It's a lemon!"

Teacher: "How about apple juice? Do you think apple juice could come out of it?"

Student: "Of course not. It's a lemon!"

Teacher: "How about grapefruit juice? Do you think grapefruit juice could come out of it?"

Student: "Of course not. It's a lemon!"

Teacher: "Tell me then, what would come out of it?"

Student: "Lemon juice, of course."

Teacher: "Why? Why is it that when you squeeze a lemon, lemon juice comes out?"

Student: "Well, it's a lemon and that's what's inside."

"What is inside becomes the outside"

Day 21

**<u>Be mindful of beliefs and thoughts - They are the only 2
things that truly hold back success in life.</u>**

Once there was a free bird. She floated in the sky, catching
midges for lunch, swam in the summer rain trickles, and was
like many other birds.

But she had a habit: every time some event occurred in her life,
whether good or bad, the bird picked up a stone from the
ground. Every day she sorted out her stones, laughed
remembering joyful events, and cried remembering the sad
ones. The bird took the stones everywhere with her, whether she
was flying high in the sky or walking on the earth. She never
forgot about them.

As the years passed, the free bird collected many more stones.
She kept on carrying them everywhere she went, remembering
the past. However, It was becoming more and more difficult to
fly, until one day she was unable to fly at all.

The bird that was once free, could no longer walk on the earth,
nor fly high in the sky. she was unable to make a move by her
own. She could not catch midges anymore; only rare rain gave
her the necessary water she needed.

The bird bravely endured all the hardships, guarding her
precious memories. After some time the bird finally died of
starvation and thirst. All that was left behind was but a bunch of
worthless stones.

*"It's the stories we tell ourselves which hold us back in life" -
Jordan Belfort*

*"The past is like an anchor holding us back. You must let go of
who you were in order to become who you will be"*

Day 22

Consistently practise doing what you fear most.

A cowardly man once visited a martial arts master and asked him to teach him bravery. The master looked at him and said:

"I will teach you with only one condition: In one month you will have to go live in a big city. On your way you are to tell every person that you meet that you are a coward. You will have to say it loudly, openly and while looking straight into the person's eyes."

The man became upset, this task was especially scary to him. For a couple of days he was very sad and thoughtful. To live with his cowardice however, was so unbearable that he travelled to the city to accomplish his mission.

At first, when meeting the people he passed by, he quailed, lost his speech and couldn't contact anyone. But he needed to finish the master's task, so he began to force himself to make more effort.

When he came upon the first passerby to tell about his cowardice, it felt to him that he would die from fear. As each day passed however his voice sounded louder and more confident. Suddenly came a day when the man caught himself thinking that he's not scared anymore.

The longer he continued doing the master's task, the more convinced he was that the fear was abandoning him. After a month had passed the man returned to the master, bowed to him and said:

"Thank you master. I have finished your task. Now I am not afraid anymore. But how did you know that this strange task will help me?

The master replied:

"The thing is that cowardice is only a habit. By continually doing the things that scare us, we can overcome old habits of thought and replace them with new brave thoughts."

"Now you know that bravery is also a habit. If you want to make bravery a part of yourself, you need to always move forward into the fear. The fear will only then go away, and bravery will take its place."

"Courage is doing what you're afraid of doing. There can be no courage unless you're afraid."

Day 23

<u>Be courageous in both actions and words</u>

I. A not so bold hunter was hunting a lion by tracking the lion's steps. He asked a woodchopper in the forest if he had seen any more of the lions tracks.

The woodchopper replied "never mind the lions tracks, I will show you to the Lion himself."

The hunter, turning very pale and with teeth chattering from fear, replied, "No, thank you. I did not ask for that, it is his tracks only that I am in search of, not the Lion himself."

II.   A young goat was perched up on the top of a house. Looking down the goat saw a wolf passing under him. Immediately he began to insult and attack his enemy.

"Murderer and thief," he cried.

"Why do you come here near honest folks' houses? How dare you make an appearance where your vile deeds are known?"

"Say as you like from a safe distance, my young friend," said the Wolf.

"Actions prove who a person is, words prove who a person wants to be"

Day 24

<u>Niceness is seen as weakness and will be exploited.</u>

I.   A small goat, returning without protection from the pasture, was being chased by a Wolf. Seeing he could not escape, he turned around, and said:

"I know that I must be your prey, but before I die I ask of you one favour. Will you play me a tune to which I may dance?"

The Wolf was nice and granted the goats one last wish. While the wolf played a song on his pipe and the Kid was dancing, some hounds hearing the sound ran up and chased the Wolf away.

The wolf thinking to himself said, "It is just what I deserve. For I am but a butcher, and should not have turned piper to please my prey."

II.   One wintry day a woodchopper was tramping home from his work when he saw something black lying on the snow. Upon closer inspection he saw it was a snake who appeared dead. He picked the snake up and held it close to his chest to warm it while he hurried home.

As soon as he got indoors he put the snake down in front of the fire. The children watched it and saw it slowly come to life again.

Then one of them stooped down to stroke it. At that very moment the snake raised its head opened its fangs about to sting the child to death. The Woodchopper seized his axe, and with one stroke cut the snake in two.

"Weakness of attitude becomes weakness of character" - Albert Einstein

"The problem with helping others first is that you've taught them that you are second"

Day 25

<u>Never reveal your weaknesses.</u>

An Eagle was soaring through the air when suddenly it heard the whizz of an Arrow, and felt itself wounded to death. Slowly it fluttered down to the earth, with its life-blood pouring out of it. Looking down upon the Arrow with which it had been pierced, it noticed that the shaft of the Arrow had been feathered with one of its own plumes.

"Alas!" it cried, "My own self has played a hand in my downfall" as it died.

"Your words and your actions will either reveal your strengths or reveal your weaknesses"

Day 26

Be decisive. A bad decision is better than no decision: A bad decision can be made right. Indecision is always wrong.

I. A great conflict was about to begin between the Birds and the Beasts.

When the two armies were collected together the Bat hesitated on which to join. The Birds that passed his perch said:

"Come with us" but he said, "I am a Beast."

Later on, some Beasts who were passing underneath him looked up and said:

"Come with us" but he said: "I am a Bird."

Luckily at the last moment peace was made, and no battle took place.

The Bat came to the Birds and wished to join in the rejoicings, but they turned against him and he found himself fleeing for his life.

He then went to the Beasts, but soon also had to retreat, for they too would have torn him to pieces.

"Ah," said the Bat, "now I understand."

II.

"Sir, What is the secret of your success?" the apprentice asked his master.

"Two words."

"And, sir, what are they?"

"Good decisions."

"And how do you make good decisions?"

"One word."

"And sir, what is that?"

"Experience."

"And how do you get Experience?"

"Two words."

"And, sir, what are they?"

"Bad decisions."

"I do not believe in taking the right decision, I take a decision and make it right." — Muhammad Ali Jinnah

"The cure for most obstacles is being decisive."

"It's not hard to make decisions once you know what your values are"

"Be decisive. A wrong decision is generally less disastrous than indecision"

Day 27

Always keep up appearances

A snake in the village had bitten so many people that few dared go into the fields. A wise master tamed the snake and persuaded it to practice the discipline of nonviolence.

It did not take long for the villagers to discover that the snake had become harmless. They took to hurling stones at it and dragging it about by its tail.

The badly battered snake crawled to the Master's house one night to complain.

The master replied, "Friend, you have stopped frightening people, that's bad!"

"But it was you who taught me to practice the discipline of nonviolence!"

"I told you to stop hurting, not to stop hissing!"

"Maintain yourself and everything maintains itself around you" - Paul Kantner

Day 28

Choose quality over quantity

A fox was taking her babies out for a walk one morning, when she came across a Lioness, with her cub in arms.

"Why such pride, haughty dame, over one solitary cub?" sneered the fox.

"Look at my healthy and numerous litter here, and imagine how much pride I must feel."

The Lioness gave her a squelching look, and lifting up her nose, while calmly walking away replied,

"Yes, just look at that beautiful collection, but what are they? Foxes! I've only one, but remember, that one is a Lion."

"Don't think of cost. Think of value."

Day 29

Hard work is the fastest short-cut to success.

A hard-working and generous farmer lived with his three lazy, greedy sons. He was elderly, and just before he died, he called them to him and told them that their inheritance was buried in his fields.

If they wished to claim it then they would have to find and dig it up. No sooner than his spirit left him than his sons went out and tore apart the fields looking for the buried treasure.

Having dug up the entire farm and found nothing, however, they began to wonder if it was a trick, and if their father, in his generosity, had already given all his money away to the poor.

One of the sons said, "Well, we've already dug the fields, we might as well sow a crop to take advantage of it." His brothers agreed, and they planted wheat in the fields, took in a good harvest, and sold it for a large sum.

After the harvest, the sons wondered if they might have just missed the treasure when digging for it, so they dug up the fields once again just in case; having found no treasure, they once again planted a crop and sold it.

This continued for a few years, until the sons had at last become accustomed to hard work.

Only then did the sons realise the valuable lesson their father had left them with on their deathbed. They became honest and content, and lived their lives in peace.

"Be stubborn about your goals, but flexible with your methods"

Day 30.

Be aware of faulty reasoning and never act upon it.

I. A donkey and a rooster were in a straw-yard together when a hungry Lion, approached.

As the lion was about to pounce upon the donkey, the rooster (The sound of whose voice the Lion is said to be averse to) crowed loudly, causing the Lion to flee as fast as he could.

The donkey, thinking the lion to thus be weak, decided to take chase in order to attack the lion.

After a short distance the Lion turned, and tore the donkey to shreds.

II.   There was once a dog whose favourite food was eggs. One day upon seeing the roundness of an Oyster, opened his mouth and swallowed it down with the utmost delight supposing it to be an egg.

Not long afterwards while suffering great pain in his stomach, he said, "I deserve this pain. It is because of my desire for all round things to be eggs that I stupidly believed it to be so."

"Same old thinking = Same old results"

Conclusion to Part 1

The true goal of knowledge is not in "knowing" but in remembering to do.

The true value of the wisdom contained within these stories will show itself if action is taken and the lessons applied to your own life. If done so, you should notice increased benefits as time passes.

At the beginning, this will require a higher than normal level of self-awareness to break old thought patterns and replace them with new.

I'd recommend seizing any opportunity you have to retell any of the stories or quotes you found useful. Not only will it benefit the listener but the retelling of the story itself will help you immensely. The act of retelling a story will deepen your understanding of the story and fix it to your own memory so much stronger.

To end this section I would like to leave you with one last quote to remember:

"Life is 10% of what happens to you and 90% of how you react to it."

Part 2: Get Happiness

Wisdom to create the mindset required for happiness

Introduction To Part 2

As an avid adventurer, it never ceases to amaze me just how happy some people are, despite their circumstances.

Lack of money, lack of food, lack of family, lack of clean living conditions, lack of health, etc. Yet unhappiness holds no place in their lives.

It is the goal of this section to impart through story and quotes, much of the wisdom and invaluable thought processes that fuel this unlimited happiness.

Happiness sits in the background of our minds waiting to be called forth. Much of the time it's pushed aside while more seemingly important things fill the space of our minds - stress, worries, anxieties, thought loops etc.

Nothing is needed to go on this adventure of increasing happiness except for an open and experimental mind.

This section (as with part one) is also deliberately suggestive and not explanatory. The purpose of which is to draw attention to your own inner thought processes.

Remember to keep each day's lesson front of mind. Each lesson is your own personal thought experiment that needs to be practised. Do this and I'm certain your overall happiness levels will increase.

Day 31

Happiness is an inside job

A beggar had been sitting by the side of the road for over thirty years. One day a stranger walked by. "Spare some change?" mumbled the beggar, mechanically holding out his old baseball cap.

"I have nothing to give you," said the stranger. Then he asked: "What's that you are sitting on?"

"Nothing," replied the beggar. "Just an old box. I have been sitting on it for as long as I can remember."

"Ever looked inside?" asked the stranger.

"No," said the beggar. "What's the point? There's nothing in there."

"Have a look inside," insisted the stranger.

The beggar pried open the lid. With astonishment, disbelief, and joy, he saw that the box was filled with gold.

"Happiness is from living life inside out" - unknown

"The primary cause of unhappiness is never the situation but your thoughts about it"

- Eckhart Tolle

Day 32

Find comfort in discomfort

A poor man lived with his wife and six children in a small one-room house. They were always getting in each other's way and there was so little space they could hardly breathe. Finally the man could stand it no more. He talked to his wife and asked her what to do. "Go and see the rabbi," she told him, and after arguing a while, he went.

The rabbi after greeting him said, "I see something is troubling you. Whatever it is, you can tell me." So the poor man told the rabbi how miserable things were in his tiny home with him, his wife, and six children all eating, living and sleeping in one room. The poor man told the rabbi, "We're now starting to yell and fight with each other. Life couldn't be worse."

The rabbi thought very deeply about the poor man's problem. Then said, "Do exactly as I tell you and things will get better. Do you promise?" "I promise," the poor man said.

The rabbi then asked the poor man a strange question. "Do you own any animals?"

"Yes," he said. "I have one cow, one goat, and some chickens." "Good," the rabbi said. "When you get home, take all the animals into your house to live with you."

The poor man was surprised to hear this strange advice from the rabbi, but he'd promised to do exactly what the rabbi said. So he went home and took all the farm animals into the tiny one-room house.

The next day the poor man ran back to see the rabbi. "What have you done to my house Rabbi?" he cried. "It's awful. I did what you told me and the animals are everywhere! Rabbi, help me!"

The rabbi listened and said calmly, "Now go home and take the chickens back outside."

The poor man did as the rabbi said, but hurried back again the next day. "The chickens are gone, but Rabbi, the goat!" he moaned. "The goat is smashing all the furniture and eating everything in sight!"

The good rabbi said, "Go home and remove the goat and may God bless you."

So the poor man went home and took the goat outside. But he ran back again to see the rabbi, crying and wailing. "What a nightmare you have brought into my house, Rabbi! With the cow it's like living in a stable! Can human beings live with an animal like this?"

The rabbi said sweetly, "My friend, you are right. May God bless you. Go home now and take the cow out of your house." And the poor man went quickly home and took the cow out of the house.

The next day he came running back to the rabbi again. "O Rabbi," he said with a big smile on his face, "we have such a good life now. The animals are all out of the house. The house is so quiet and we've got room to spare! What a joy!"

"As the valley gives height to the mountain, so too does discomfort give meaning to pleasure"

A happy life consists not in the absence, but in the mastery of hardships" - Hellen Keller

Day 33

Sacrifice what's good to achieve what's great

There was once a successful businessman who had everything – a beautiful wife, adorable children and a big house in which they all lived happily. The pride of his life though was his exotic songbird which he kept in a cage and fed delicious titbits when it entertained his guests.

One day the man had to go on a journey faraway and he asked his wife and children what presents they would like from abroad – they asked for fine silks, honeycomb and clockwork toys. Finally he asked his songbird if he would like him to bring anything back.

"I ask only for one small favour." The songbird replied.

"Anything!" his master declared.

"Just this – when you see my cousins in the trees in the place you're going to, please tell them about my conditions here."

"Are you sure? I could bring you back a fine jewel-encrusted mirror or dried tropical fruit?"

"No, just this, thank you." The songbird replied and the man went away feeling a little disconcerted but decided to carry out his pet's wishes.

The man made his trip safely and successfully concluded his business. He spent his remaining time buying the presents as his family had requested. Finally, he went to a park and saw some birds in the trees that bore a remarkable resemblance to his own songbird. He called up to one of them and told them about how his own bird lived in cage and sang for him.

No sooner had he finished speaking than one of these exotic birds trembled on its perch and tumbled to the ground and ceased to move. The man held his head in grief and the incident quite spoiled his trip.

He returned home and greeted his wife and family who were delighted at their presents. He couldn't share their pleasure however as as the forthcoming encounter with his songbird remained on his conscience. Finally he found the courage to go down to the garden.

"Well?" his songbird asked and, hesitantly, the man told him exactly what had happened. The song bird listened intently, then trembled on his perch and fell to the bottom of his cage, dead.

The man was now beside himself with grief and confusion. Weeping openly, he opened the door of the cage and carried out his beloved songbird in his hands. No sooner had he done so, however, that his songbird returned to life and flew up to the branches of the nearest tree. The let out a shrill of joy at finding its freedom.

The man scratched his head confused and eventually asked:

"Okay, you win. But tell me please, what was in the message that contained this trick?"

The songbird looked down at him with pity and said "My cousin showed me that it was my beauty that kept me in the cage. Were it not for the delight of my singing voice you would have lost interest long ago. I had to give up that life in order to become free."

"Don't be afraid to give up the good to go for what's great" - John D. Rockefeller

Day 34

The grass is not greener on the other side. It's greener wherever you water it

There was once a stonemason who was dissatisfied with himself and with his position in life.

One day he passed a wealthy merchant's house. Through the open gateway, he saw many fine possessions and important visitors. "How powerful that merchant must be!" thought the stonemason. He became envious and wished with all his might that he could become like the merchant.

To his great surprise, he suddenly became the merchant, enjoying more luxuries and power than he had ever imagined. However he soon found that he was envied and detested by those less wealthy than himself. Soon a high official passed by, carried in a chair, accompanied by attendants and escorted by soldiers beating gongs. Everyone, no matter how wealthy, had to bow low before the procession. "How powerful being an official is!" he thought. "I wish that I could be a high official!"

He then became the high official, carried everywhere high above others in his embroidered chair, while being feared and hated by people all around. It was a hot summer day, and the official found himself feeling uncomfortable in his sticky chair. He looked up at the sun. It shone proudly in the sky, unaffected by his presence. "How powerful the sun is!" he thought. "I wish that I could be the sun!"

He then became the sun, shining fiercely down on everyone, scorching the fields, cursed by the farmers and laborers. A huge black cloud then moved between him and the earth, so that his light could no longer shine on everything below. "How powerful that storm cloud is!" he thought. "I wish that I could be a cloud!"

He then became the cloud, flooding the fields and villages, shouted at by everyone. However he soon found that he was being pushed away by some greater force, and realized that it was the wind. "How powerful the wind is!" he thought. "I wish that I could be the wind!"

He then became the wind, blowing tiles off the roofs of houses, uprooting trees, feared and hated by all below him. But after a while, he ran up against something that would not move, no matter how forcefully he blew against it – a huge, towering rock. "How powerful that rock is!" he thought. "I wish I could be a rock!"

He then became the rock, more powerful than anything else on earth. But as he stood there, he heard the sound of a hammer pounding a chisel into his hard surface, and felt himself being changed. "What could be more powerful than I, the rock?" he thought.

He looked down and saw far below him the figure of a stonemason.

"To keep chasing the reward at the end of the rainbow is to burn your toast"

"He that finds discontentment in one place is not likely to find happiness in another"

Day 35

<u>Focus on what you have, not on what you don't have.</u>

I.

A church was being built in a small village. Each day the village children would come to help. None of the kids owned shoes but one happy little boy always wore one sock. No shoes, just a single sock. He was nicknamed One-Sock.

One day one of the builders curiously asked, "One-Sock, tell me about this one sock you wear." One-Sock proudly replied, "Every night my mum washes it and I wear it every day."

"Yes, but why wear just one?", the builder queried.

One-Sock, surprised by the builder's silly question, smiled broadly and replied, "Because I only have one!"

"You will never reach your destination if you stop and throw rocks at every dog that barks" - Winston Churchill

"It is not the man who has too little, but the man who craves more, that is poor. " – Seneca

II.

A successful business owner was invited to address a group of young students on the subject of opportunities.

He started his talk by tacking a big sheet of white paper to the class room wall and placing a black dot in the middle of the sheet.

"What do you see?" he asked, pointing to the paper on the wall. "A black spot," was the reply from most in the audience.

"Yes, I see a black spot too," replied the businessman, "but none of you saw the much greater area of white. This is the point of my talk on perspective."

"You get what you focus on, so focus on what you want"

Day 36

Take Leaps of Faith

A climber found himself lost as night fell in the heights of the mountain. All he could see was black everywhere with the moon and stars nowhere to be found. Being close to the top of the mountain he continued climbing. Suddenly he slipped and fell, falling at great speed. All he felt was a terrible sensation of being sucked down by gravity.

As he kept falling, all the good and bad moments of his life passed before his eyes. He then began thinking about how death was quickly approaching, when all of a sudden the rope tied to his waist pull him hard. His body lay hanging in the air.

Only the rope was holding him and in that moment of stillness he had no other choice but to scream "Help me God."

A deep voice coming from the sky answered, "What is it you want me to do?" "Save me God." And God replied "Do you really think I can save you?" "Of course, I believe You can."

"Then cut the rope tied to your waist" was God's reply.

There was a moment of great silence.....As the man pondered. He decided to hold onto the rope with all his strength.

The next morning a rescue team found the climber, dead and frozen, his body hanging from a rope. His hands holding tight onto the rope, one foot away from the ground.

"All beliefs are leaps of faith, it's just some are larger than others"

"Leap and the net will appear" - Zen Proverb

Day 37

We are all imperfect. Strive for improvement

A poor man was caught stealing a loaf of bread and was ordered to be hanged by the king. On the way to his execution he told the guard, that he knew a wonderful secret, and that it would be a shame for the secret to die with him.

The guard listened as the poor man requested to tell his secret in front of the king. The man revealed that his secret would allow a person to bury the seed of a date palm which would grow and bear fruit overnight.

The guard enthralled by this possibility, brought the poor man before the governor, who presented him to the King's high officers of state and the King himself. Standing before these powerful men, the poor man dug a hole in the ground and said, "This is the secret. This seed can only be planted by a person who has never stolen or taken anything which did not belong to him. I am unable to plant this seed."

The poor man turned to the governor who, frightened, revealed that in his younger days he had retained something that wasn't his.

The thief then turned to the treasurer who said that it was probable while dealing with such large sums of money, he might have at some point entered too much or too little.

Finally the thief turned to the king, who embarrassingly admitted to keeping a bracelet of his father's without his blessing.

The poor man then said, "You are all mighty and powerful men, none of whom lack material comfort, and yet none of you can plant this seed. While I who have stolen but a single loaf of bread due to starvation am to be hanged" The king, pleased with the shrewdness of the poor man, pardoned him.

"Forget what we became, focus on what we're capable of becoming." - Aniekee Tochukwu Ezekiel

Day 38

It is impossible to win 100% of the time.

A man was speeding down the highway, feeling safe in a group of cars traveling at the same speed. They soon passed a speed-trap, and he found himself being pulled over by a police officer.

The officer handed him the fine, and was about to walk away when the man asked, "Officer, I know I was speeding, but it's not fair. There were plenty of other cars around me who were going just as fast, if not faster, so why did I get the ticket?"

"Ever go fishing?" the policeman asked the man.

"Well, yeah, of course I go fishing all the time," the man replied.

The officer grinned and added, "Well do you ever catch all the fish?"

"Sometimes you win, sometimes you learn"

"There is such a thin line between winning and losing" - John R. Tunis

Day 39

Thoughts held onto carry a heavy weight on happiness

Two monks were out for a walk one day. One older, the other much younger. They had both taken vows of silence and chastity. As they continued along the trail, they came to a creek where they saw a girl standing on the bank, she told them that she needed to get across.

Without hesitation the older monk picked her up in his arms and waded across the creek with her. Once they both got to the other side, they went on their way.

An hour on down the trail the younger of the two broke his vow of silence, "You know with our vow of chastity we are not to even touch a woman, let alone make eye contact with one!"

The older one, who had been admiring the beauty of the woods and the songs of the birds, replied, "Brother, I set her down on the bank an hour ago. You, however, are still carrying her."

"Don't carry what you don't need, in your pocket, in your home or in your head"

"Feelings are just visitors, let them come and go"

Day 40

Life is how you make it

I.

A trader was travelling across the Desert with his workers and camels. As the night set in, they decided to set up camp for the night. As the workers drove their pegs into the ground to secure the camels they found themselves one peg short. "There are only nineteen pegs and we've got twenty camels. How do we tie the twentieth camel?" the workers asked the trader.

The trader replied "These camels are stupid animals. Just go through the motions of tying the camel and he'll stay put all night," which is what they did. The twentieth camel then stood there as if bound to the invisible peg.

The next morning the worker packed their tents and pegs to continue their journey. As they were leaving they noticed all the camels were following except the twentieth one. It refused to budge despite the workers best efforts. They then asked the trader who said, "You forgot to untie him."

The workers replied "Oh, yes," so they went through the motions of untying him and along on the journey they went.

II.

A man was once found wandering the desert in swimming trunks and towel in hand. He came upon an Arab and greets him. The Arab replies with a hello.

"How far away from here is the sea?" the man asks the Arab.

"The sea? For heaven's sake," says the Arab, "that's a thousand miles away from here." The man in trunks replies, "Boy, some beach you guys have out here!"

"Invisible chains are those which weigh most heavily"

"With our thoughts we make the world" – Buddha

Day 41

Life is a series of seasons. Each season makes way for the next

There was a man who had four sons. He wanted his sons to learn to not judge things too quickly. So he sent them each on a quest, in turn, to go and look at a pear tree that was a great distance away. The first son went in the winter, the second in the spring, the third in summer, and the youngest son in the fall.

When they had all gone and come back, he called them together to describe what they had seen. The first son said that the tree was ugly, bent, and twisted.

The second son said no – it was covered with green buds and full of promise.

The third son disagreed, he said it was laden with blossoms that smelled so sweet and looked so beautiful, it was the most graceful thing he had ever seen.

The last son disagreed with all of them; he said it was ripe and drooping with fruit, full of life and fulfilment.

The man then explained to his sons that they were all right, because they had each seen but one season in the tree's life. He told them that you cannot judge a tree, or a person, by only one season, and that the essence of who they are – and the pleasure, joy, and love that come from that life – can only be measured at the end, when the fruit is born.

"Nothing is permanent. Everything is subject to change. Being is always becoming" – Buddha

Day 42

Unhappiness arises from dwelling on the past and anticipating the future

One day, while walking through the wilderness, a man encountered a vicious tiger. He ran for his life, and the tiger gave chase. The man came to the edge of a cliff, and the tiger was almost upon him. Having no choice, he held onto a vine with both hands and climbed down.

Halfway down the cliff, the man looked up and saw the tiger at the top, baring its fangs. He looked down and saw another tiger at the bottom, roaring, eagerly awaiting his arrival. He was caught between the two.

Two wild rats, soon appeared on the vine above him and soon started gnawing on the vine. He knew that as the rats kept chewing away, they would reach a point when the vine would no longer be able to support his weight. It'd break and he would fall. He tried to shoo the rats away but alas they kept coming back.

At that moment, he noticed a strawberry growing on the face of the cliff, not far away from him. It looked plump and ripe. Holding onto the vine with one hand, he reached out and plucked it.

With the tiger above, another below, and two rats continuing to gnaw on his vine, the man was able to fully appreciate the strawberry. Upon tasting it, he found it to be the most delicious meal he had ever had.

"Realize deeply that the present moment is all you ever have. Make the Now the primary focus of your life." - Eckhart Tolle.

"Begin at once to live, and count each separate day as a separate life." – Seneca

Day 43

Change the frame through which you see the world

A seeker of happiness was told to visit a well inside of cave. Ask the well what is truth he was told by a wise man, and the well will tell you. After finding the well, the seeker asked his most important question to which the well replied "visit the village crossroad and there you will find what you are seeking."

Full of hope the man ran to the crossroad to find three rather uninteresting shops. One shop sold pieces of metal, another sold wood, and the third sold thin wires. None of these things he believed had anything to do with the attainment of happiness.

Disappointed, the seeker returned to the well to demand an explanation, but he was told only, "In time you will understand." The man protested but only received echoes of his voice in reply. Annoyed for having been made a fool of (or so he believed at the time) the seeker continued his search for truth. His memory of the well faded as the years went by. One night, while he was walking in the moonlight, the sound of guitar music caught his attention. It was wonderful music played with great mastery and inspiration.

Moved by the beautiful music the seeker approached the guitar player noticing his fingers dancing over the strings. He then became aware of the guitar itself. All of a sudden it came to him in a moment of joyous recognition. The guitar was made out of wires and pieces of metal and wood just as he had seen in the three stores.

At last he understood the message of the well: all that we need to be happy is already within us. It is our task is to assemble and use our mind in the appropriate way. As soon as we assemble our mind in a certain fashion happiness is born.

"You can change the world by changing how you see it"

Day 44

Increasing happiness is not a process of addition, it's a process of subtraction

There is a story about a man who had a huge boulder in his front yard. He grew weary of this big, unattractive stone in the centre of his lawn, so he decided to take advantage of it and turn it into an object of art.

He went to work on it with hammer and chisel, and chipped away at the huge boulder until it became a beautiful stone elephant. When he finished, it was gorgeous, breath-taking.

A neighbor asked, "How did you ever carve such a marvelous likeness of an elephant?"

The man answered, "I just chipped away everything that didn't look like an elephant!"

Perfection is achieved, not when there is nothing more to add, but when there is nothing left to take away. - Antoine de Saint-Exupery

Day 45

External circumstance need not affect inner tranquility

There once lived a great warrior. Though quite old, he still was able to defeat any challenger. His reputation extended far and wide throughout the land and many students gathered to study under him.

One day an infamous young warrior arrived at the village. He was determined to be the first man to defeat the great master. Along with his strength, he had an uncanny ability to spot and exploit any weakness in an opponent. He would wait for his opponent to make the first move, thus revealing a weakness, and then would strike with merciless force and lightning speed. No one had ever lasted with him in a match beyond the first move.

Much against the advice of his worried students, the old master gladly accepted the young warrior's challenge. As the two squared off for battle, the young warrior began to hurl insults at the old master. He threw dirt and spit in his face. For hours he verbally assaulted him with every curse and insult known to mankind. But the old warrior merely stood there motionless and calm. Finally, the young warrior exhausted himself. Knowing he was defeated, he left feeling shamed.

Somewhat disappointed that their master did not fight the insolent youth directly, the students gathered around the old master and questioned him. "How could you endure such an indignity? How did you drive him away?"

"If someone comes to give you a gift and you do not receive it," the master replied, "to whom does the gift belong?"

"The giver" the students replied. It was then that the students understood. The young warrior was defeated not by the old master but by his very own insults.

"It is the power of the mind to be unconquerable." - Seneca

"People are not disturbed by things, but by the view they take of them" Epictetus

Day 46

Accept that which is out of our control and improve that which is in our control

There was once a woman who spent the whole autumn sowing and preparing her garden. In the spring, her flowers bloomed and blossomed. However on closer inspection she noticed a few flowering weeds she had not planted.

As quickly as she removed the weeds, more seemed to take their place. The seeds had already spread. She searched for a weed killer that would kill only the type of weeds she had, but was unsuccessful. The more she learnt the more it became apparent that all of the various weedkillers available would end up killing her beautiful flowers as well. At the end of her rope she sought the help of her more experienced friend.

Her friend explained "It's just like marriage, along with all the good things, there are always a few bad things we cannot change."

"What should I do, then?" the lady asked.

"Nothing. They may not be the flowers you wanted to have, but they are a part of the garden."

"Life is a balance of holding on and letting go"

Day 47

Happiness is not found in the same place it was lost

One day an old alley cat crossed paths with a younger cat who was frantically running around, trying to catch its own tail. The older cat watched curiously for awhile. When the young cat stopped for a rest, the older cat asked, "Would you mind telling me what you are doing?"

The young cat said, "Sure, I went to Cat Philosophy School and learnt that happiness is found in our tails. I plan to keep chasing my tail knowing that someday I will catch it and get a big bite of happiness."

The older cat amused, replied, "Well, I've never been to Cat Philosophy School, but I agree, happiness is most definitely in our tails. However, I have found that when I just wander around enjoying life, it follows me everywhere I go."

"The truth is, you can skip the pursuit of happiness altogether and just be happy" -Joshua Fields Millburn

"The pursuit of happiness ends when you realise that you are happiness"

Day 48

"Need" nothing

A wise man's follower once asked, "You said that no desire, no action. no virtue, no truth are the Four Laws to Peace and Joy. But I do not see how there can be joy when there is no existence."

The wise master, answered, "What a wonderful question. I will tell you again. It is only nothing that can give rise to something. If it were in something, peace and joy would never be."

"Why?" you may ask. Take for example a mountain filled with forest. The leaves and branches of the trees spread shade everywhere. Surely this mountain forest does not seek birds and animals, but they all come here on their own to nest and gather.

"Or think of a great sea that draws all the rivers and springs and is vast without limits and deep beyond measure, Surely this ocean does not seek fish and scaly creatures. But they all dwell there on their own.

"Those of you who seek Peace and Joy are like these birds and fish. You need only pacify your minds and live quietly. Then in practicing these teachings, you will not have to seek Peace and Joy, they will simply be there like the forest and the ocean.This is how nothing gives rise to something."

"Needing nothing attracts everything" - Russell Simmons

"The greatest wealth is a poverty of desires" – Seneca

Day 49

Whatever the current situation is, accept it as if you had chosen it

A proud and well presented old lady was preparing to move into a nursing home for the first time.

She smiled graciously as the orderly advised her that her room was now ready. The orderly gave her a description of her new small room in detail as she slowly followed along beside her.

"I love it," she stated with the enthusiasm of an eight-year-old.

"But dear, you haven't even seen your room yet.... just wait" replied the orderly.

"That doesn't have anything to do with it," the elderly woman replied.

"Happiness is something I decide on ahead of time. Whether I like my room or not doesn't depend on how the furniture is arranged ... it's how I arrange my mind. I already decided to love it and so it shall be"

"Happiness is an attitude. We either make ourselves miserable, or happy and strong. The amount of work is the same" - Francesca Reigler

"Judge nothing, you will be happy. Forgive everyone, you will be happier. Love everything, you will be happiest."

"There are only two ways to live your life. One is as though nothing is a miracle, and the other is as though everything is a miracle" - Albert Einstein

Day 50

The quality of your decisions equals the quality of your life

The farmers apprentice was eager to learn about agriculture and so called upon the farmer

"How's the wheat coming along dear sir?" to which the farmer replied, "I didn't plant any."

"Really?" asked his apprentice surprised. "I thought this was the season to plant wheat"

"For most farmers it is" was the farmers reply. "However I'm afraid we might not have enough rain this year."

"Well, how about your corn? How is it doing?" the young man queried.

"Didn't plant corn this year either" the farmer replied. "I'm concerned about corn diseases"

"Alfalfa?"

"No. I'm Afraid the price might drop."

"Well, then," asked the now confused apprentice "what did you plant?"

"Nothing," the farmer replied. "I played it safe."

"May your choices reflect your hopes, not your fears" - Nelson Mandela

Day 51

Stay Humble, stay grounded

Long ago, in a hermitage, there lived a great sage. One day, as he sat down to have his lunch, a mouse fell from the beak of a crow, on the ground near him. He picked the mouse up, took him inside the ashram and fed him some rice.

One day, the sage saw a cat chasing the mouse around the ashram. He was afraid that his pet mouse would be killed by the cat. By the power of his penance, he turned the mouse into a cat so that it could defend itself against other cats.

Soon a dog appeared on the scene and started barking at and chasing the cat. When the sage saw this, he changed the cat into a dog.

One day his dog was frightened by a tiger. The sage immediately changed his dog into a tiger, again by the power of his penance.

However, the sage always treated the tiger as if it was still his little mouse. Whenever the villagers who passed by the sage's ashram saw the tiger, they would say, "Ha! That's not a tiger! It's just a mouse that the sage changed into a tiger. He won't eat us or even scare us."

When the tiger heard this, he was furious. "As long as the sage is alive," he thought,"the truth about my real nature will never die. I must get rid of him for good."The tiger decided to kill the sage but as soon as the sage saw him coming towards him, he knew what was going on in the tiger's mind. He shouted, "Get back into your form of a mouse."

No sooner had he uttered these words than the tiger shrank and became a little mouse once again. The sage looked at him with pity and said, "Whatever one is, large or small, it's good to be humble."

"Humility is not thinking less of yourself, it is thinking of yourself less" - C.S. Lewis

Day 52

Pay attention to the things you are not paying attention to

A wise zen master was visiting the city and walking on a busy street with one of his students. There was much noise in the city; car horns, feet shuffling, and people talking. Despite the noise, the zen master turned to his student suddenly and said, "I hear a cricket" his eyes beaming with wonder and surprise.

"No, that's impossible" his student replied. "How could you hear a cricket with all of this noise? You must be imagining it. Besides, I've never seen a cricket in the city."

"No really, I hear a cricket. I will show you." The master paused for a moment, then led his student across the street to a big cement planter with a tree in it. Pushing back the leaves he uncovered a little brown cricket.

"That's amazing!" said his student. "You must have super-human hearing. What's your secret?"

"No, my hearing is just the same as yours. There's no secret," The master replied. "

The master then reached into his bag, pulled out some loose change, and threw it on the sidewalk. Amid all of the noise of the city, everyone within thirty feet turned their head to see where the sound of the money was coming from.

"See," he said. "It's all a matter of what you are listening for."

"What you pay attention to, becomes you"

Day 53

Learn to let go

In India the local monkey catchers have perfected a particular method to catch monkeys to sell as pets to wealthy families. The monkey catchers dig a small hole in the ground in which they place fruits and nuts.

They then cover this hole with a wooden plank with a hole in it. The hole is just large enough to allow the monkey to put their arm through in order to grab the food.

The catchers wait patiently for the monkeys to come along, lured by the delicious smell of the sweet fruits and nuts. The monkey then sticks his arm in the hole and wraps his hand around the treats forming a fist. However the fist full of treats will not fit out of the hole. Only an empty hand can be pulled out.

When the Catchers approach the monkeys they often scramble around attempting to get out but will refuse to let go of the treats. Even as the net is thrown over the monkey and the monkey is picked up and placed in a sack does the monkey not let go of their grip on the treats.

If only the monkeys had learnt to let go they could have easily escaped. This is especially so considering the fruits and nuts are easily be found in their surroundings.

"If you want to grow, you must learn to let go" - Darren Johnson

"Learn to let go, that is the key to happiness" - Buddha

Day 54

You attract that which you "are" not that which you "want"

A monastery had fallen on hard times. It was once part of a great order which, as a result of religious persecution lost all its branches. It was decimated to the extent that there were only five monks left in the mother house: the Abbot and four others, all of whom were over seventy. Clearly it was a dying order.

Deep in the woods surrounding the monastery was a little hut that the Rabbi from a nearby town occasionally used for a hermitage. One day, it occurred to the Abbot to visit the hermitage to see if the Rabbi could offer any advice that might save the monastery. The Rabbi welcomed the Abbot and commiserated. "I know how it is" he said, "the spirit has gone out of people. Almost no one comes to the synagogue anymore." So the old Rabbi and the old Abbot wept together, and spoke quietly of deep things.

The time came when the Abbot had to leave. They embraced. "It has been wonderful being with you," said the Abbot, "but I have failed in my purpose for coming. Have you no piece of advice that might save the monastery?" "No, I am sorry," the Rabbi responded, "I have no advice to give. The only thing I can tell you is that the Messiah is one of you."

When the other monks heard the Rabbi's words, they wondered what possible significance they might have. "The Messiah is one of us? One of us, here, at the monastery? Do you suppose he meant the Abbot? Of course – it must be the Abbot, who has been our leader for so long. On the other hand, he might have meant Brother

Thomas, who is undoubtedly a holy man. Certainly he couldn't have meant Brother Elrod – he's so grumpy. But then Elrod is

83

very wise. Surely, he could not have meant Brother Phillip – he's too passive. But then, magically, he's always there when you need him. Of course he didn't mean me – yet supposing he did? Oh Lord, not me! I couldn't mean that much to you, could I?"

As they contemplated in this manner, the old monks began to treat each other with extraordinary respect, on the off chance that one of them might be the Messiah. And on the off off chance that each monk himself might be the Messiah, they began to treat themselves with extraordinary respect.

Because the forest in which the monastery was situated was beautiful, people occasionally came to visit the monastery, to picnic or to wander along the old paths, most of which led to the dilapidated chapel. They sensed the aura of extraordinary respect and kindness that surrounded the five old monks, permeating the atmosphere.

They began to come more frequently, bringing their friends, and their friends brought friends. Some of the younger men who came to visit began to engage in conversation with the monks. After a while, one asked if he might join. Then another, and another. Within a few years, the monastery became once again a thriving order, and – thanks to the Rabbi's gift – a vibrant community of light and love.

"What you think you feel, what you feel you attract, what you imagine you create" - Buddha

Day 55

Do not avoid obstacles, overcome them

In ancient times, a King had a boulder placed on a roadway. Then he hid himself and watched to see if anyone would remove the huge rock. Some of the king's wealthiest merchants and courtiers came by and simply walked around it. Many loudly blamed the King for not keeping the roads clear, but no one did anything about getting the stone out of the way.

Then a peasant came along carrying a load of vegetables. Upon approaching the boulder, the peasant laid down his burden and tried to move the stone to the side of the road. After much pushing and straining, he finally succeeded.

After the peasant picked up his load of vegetables, he noticed a purse lying in the road where the boulder had been. The purse contained many gold coins and a note from the King indicating that the gold was for the person who removed the boulder from the roadway.

"An obstacle is often a stepping stone"

"Obstacles are opportunities in disguise"

"That which we resist the most is often what we need to do the most"

Day 56

Practise the art of giving

A little boy about 10 years old was standing before a shoe store on the roadway, barefooted, peering through the window, and shivering with cold. A lady approached the boy and said, "My little fellow, why are you looking so earnestly in that window?"

"I was asking God to give me a pair of shoes," was the boy's reply.

The lady took him by the hand and went into the store and asked the clerk to get half a dozen pairs of socks for the boy. She then asked if he could give her a basin of water and a towel. He quickly brought them to her. She took the little fellow to the back part of the store and, removing her gloves, knelt down, washed his little feet, and dried them with a towel.

By this time the clerk had returned with the socks. Placing a pair upon the boy's feet, she purchased him a pair of shoes. She tied up the remaining pairs of socks and gave them to him. She patted him on the head and said, "No doubt, my little fellow, you feel more comfortable now?"

As she turned to go, the astonished lad caught her by the hand, and looking up in her face, with tears his eyes, answered the question with these words: "Are you God's Wife?"

"Doing good, does you good"

"The happiest people are not those who are getting more but those who are giving more"

Day 57

All endings are beginnings

There was a shipwreck and only one man survived, cast ashore on a tiny island with nothing but the clothes on his back. For a while he hoped for rescue. But in time he knew he had to make a life there on the island.

He taught himself to fish and hunt, to garden and cook, and he built himself a charming little cottage overlooking the bay. He even carved a tiny flute which he played every night after supper.

One day he hiked to the top of the mountain at the centre of the island to see what he could see. As he reached the top, what he saw was a tower of smoke and his little cottage going up in flames.

He ran down the mountain as fast as he could. But it was too late. The cottage was in ashes – and his flute, his garden, his tools, his bow and arrows – everything he'd made with his own hands was gone, all gone!

He wept. He raged. He cursed God. He despaired. And finally, as night came, he collapsed on the sand and fell into a deep sleep.

The next morning he was awakened by sailors who had rowed ashore from a great ship to rescue him. "But," he exclaimed, "how after all this time did you know I was here?"

"Ah," said the captain, "we saw the smoke from your signal fire."

"New beginnings are often disguised as painful endings" - Lao Tzu

Day 58

Choose the lighter side of life

A rabbi went on a journey with his servant named Jacob. Their cart was drawn by a lively horse of which the rabbi was very fond. When they came to a roadside inn, the rabbi went in to rest, leaving his horse in Jacob's care.

In the meantime, a horse trader passed by and, seeing Jacob, soon made friends with him. He plied him with drink and Jacob soon was so intoxicated it was easy for the horse trader to induce him to sell him the horse for a song. Although drunk, Jacob was frightened by what he had done. What would the rabbi say when he came out of the inn?

An idea occurred to him. He placed himself between the empty shafts of the cart and started to chew hay. When the rabbi came out, he was struck speechless by what he saw."What's the meaning of this?" he finally managed to stammer. "Where's the horse?"

"The horse? That's me!" replied Jacob, and he uttered a loud whinny.

"What on earth are you doing?" murmured the confused rabbi, "Have you gone out of your mind?"

"Don't be angry with me, Rabbi," pleaded his servant Jacob. "Years ago a great misfortune happened to me. I was a young man then, a little wild and foolish, and, may God forgive me, I sinned with a woman. So to punish me, God turned me into a horse – your horse. For twenty long years you have been my master, Rabbi, little suspecting who I really was. Well, it seems my punishment is over. I'm again a man, praise God!"

When the rabbi heard Jacob's story he began to tremble and prayed for God's mercy. However, there was a practical difficulty to attend to – he could not continue his journey without a horse, so he went into the market place to buy one.

Suddenly, he stood face to face with his old horse. It was munching a wisp of hay at the horse trader's. Going up to it in alarm, the rabbi whispered into its ear, "For goodness sake, Jacob! Again, so soon!"

"Life is too important to be taken seriously" - Oscar wilde

"Laugh and the world laughs with you, weep and you weep alone"

Day 59

Apply the test of three to conversations

"Socrates, do you know what I just heard about one of your students?" "Wait a moment," Socrates replied. "Before you tell me, I'd like you to pass a little test. It's called the Test of Three."

"Test of Three?" "That's correct," Socrates continued. "Before you talk to me about my student let's take a moment to test what you're going to say. The first test is Truth. Have you made absolutely sure that what you are about to tell me is true?" "No," the man replied, "actually I just heard about it."

"All right," said Socrates. "So you don't really know if it's true or not. Now let's try the second test, the test of Goodness. Is what you are about to tell me about my student something good?" "No, on the contrary…" So," Socrates continued, "you want to tell me something bad about him even though you're not certain it's true?" The man shrugged, a little embarrassed.

Socrates continued, "You may still pass though, because there is a third test—the filter of Usefulness. Is what you want to tell me about my student going to be useful to me?" "No, not really…"

"Well," concluded Socrates, "if what you want to tell me is neither True nor Good nor even Useful, why tell it to me at all?" The man was both defeated and ashamed and said no more.

"Speak only if it improves upon the silence" - Buddha

"Poisonous people do not deserve your time, to think otherwise is masochistic" - Tim Ferriss

"If you propose to speak always ask yourself, is it true? is it necessary? is it kind? – Buddha

Day 60

Create your day, design your life

A boat docked in a tiny Mexican village.

An American tourist complimented the Mexican fisherman on the quality of his fish and asked how long it took him to catch them."Not very long," answered the Mexican.

"But then, why didn't you stay out longer and catch more?" asked the American.The Mexican explained that his small catch was sufficient to meet his needs and those of his family.

The American asked, "But what do you do with all your time?""I sleep late, fish a little, play with my children, and take a siesta with my wife. In the evenings, I go into the village to see my friends, have a few drinks, play the guitar, and sing a few songs...I have a full life."

The American interrupted, "I have a degree in business management and I can help you!"

You should start by fishing longer every day. You can then sell the extra fish you catch. With the extra revenue, you can buy a bigger boat. With the extra money the larger boat will bring, you can buy a second one and a third one and so on until you have an entire fleet of trawlers.

Instead of selling your fish to a middle man, you can negotiate directly with the processing plants and maybe even open your own plant. You can then leave this little village and move to Mexico City, Los Angeles, or even New York City! From there you can direct your huge enterprise."

"How long would that take?" asked the Mexican.

"Twenty, perhaps twenty-five years," replied the American. "And after that?"

"Afterwards? That's when it gets really interesting," answered the American, laughing. "When your business gets really big, you can start selling stock and make millions!"

"Millions? Really? And after that?"

"After that – and this is the best part – you'll be able to retire, live in a tiny village near the coast, sleep late, catch a few fish, take a siesta, and spend your evenings drinking and enjoying your friends!"

"Design your own life, create your own happiness"

"The purpose of life is to live a life of purpose" - Richard Leider

"Excitement is the more practical synonym for happiness, and it is precisely what you should strive to chase. Boredom is the opposite of happiness" - Tim Ferriss

"Happiness is not something ready-made, it comes from your own actions" - Dalai Lama

Conclusion

We have now come to the end of your 60 day journey. I sincerely hope that these stories have helped change any faulty thought processes you may have and perhaps inspire a new mindset and outlook on life.

When it comes to leading a happy life, I believe the question we should be asking is not: "what do I want?" or "what are my goals?" but "what excites me? If we are continually challenging ourselves while doing that which truly excites us happiness will always be a byproduct.

In closing, I would like to leave you with one last important quote to remember:

"Happiness does not depend on what you have or who you are. It solely relies on how you think."- Buddha

43293589R00057

Made in the USA
San Bernardino, CA
17 December 2016